The Heinemann Illustrated Encyclopedia

Volume 6
Lib-Net

First published in Great Britain by Heinemann Library
Halley Court, Jordan Hill, Oxford OX2 8EJ
a division of Reed Educational and Professional Publishing Ltd.

OXFORD MELBOURNE AUCKLAND
JOHANNESBURG BLANTYRE GABORONE
IBADAN PORTSMOUTH NH (USA) CHICAGO

Series Editors: Rebecca and Stephen Vickers
Author Team: Rob Alcraft, Catherine Chambers, Jim Drake,
Fred Martin, Angela Royston, Jane Shuter, Roger Thomas,
Rebecca Vickers, Stephen Vickers
Reading Consultant: Betty Root

Photo research by Katharine Smith
Designed and Typeset by Gecko Ltd
Printed in Hong Kong by Wing King Tong

02 01 00 99 98
10 9 8 7 6 5 4 3 2 1

ISBN 0 431 09057 2

British Library Cataloguing in Publication Data.

The Heinemann illustrated encyclopedia
1. Children's encyclopedias and dictionaries
I. Vickers, Rebecca II. Vickers, Stephen, 1951–
032

ISBN 0431090629

Acknowledgements:
Cover: The cover illustration is of a male specimen of *Ornithoptera goliath*, commonly called the
Goliath Birdwing. Special thanks to Dr George C. McGavin and the Hope Entomological
Collections, Oxford University Museum of Natural History.

J. Allan Cash Ltd: pp4, 14, 7, 27, 47, 48. **Bridgeman Art Library:** pp8t, 28. **John Cleare Mountain
Camera:** p19. **Trevor Clifford Photography:** p21b. **Chris Honeywell:** p24t. **Bruce Coleman:**
Alain Compost – p18b, Jeff Foot – 31b. **Corbis-Bettman:** p45. **Michael Holford/British
Museum:** p10b. **Hulton Getty:** p40b. **The Hutchison Library:** Bernard Regent – p36. **Oxford
Scientific Film:** p5b, Waina Cheng – p11t, J.A.L. Cooke - p37t, Kenneth Day – p20b, Michael
Fogden – p22, David C Fritts – p33b, Mike Hill – p33t, Michael Leach – p42b, Zig Leszczynski –
p30b, Renee Lynn – p9t, Fred McConnaughey – p31t, John Mitchell – p39t, Lloyd Nielsen – p20t,
Stan Osolinski – p35, Peter Parks – p5t, Keith Ringland – p29, Norbert Rosing – p9b, Frithjof Skibbe
– p38, Michael R. Stoklos – p8b, Survival Anglia – p15 (Doug Allan), p41 (Daniel Vall), K.G.Vock –
p39b, Barrie E. Watts – pp18t, 42t, W. Wisniewski – p11b. **Redferns:** pp43, 4. **Science Photo
Library:** David Guyon – p24b, Pekka Parvianen – p26b, John Sandford – p26t. **Stock Market:**
p7b. **Tony Stone Worldwide:** Byron Jorjorian – p7t, Reg Watson – p23. **Zefa:** p40t.

Every effort has been made to contact copyright holders of any material
reproduced in this book. Any omissions will be rectified in subsequent printings
if notice is given to the Publisher.

Welcome to the
Heinemann Illustrated Encyclopedia

What is an encyclopedia?

An encyclopedia is an information book. It gives the most important facts about a lot of different subjects. This encyclopedia has been specially written for children your age. It covers many of the subjects from school and others you may find interesting.

What is in this encyclopedia?

In this encyclopedia each topic is called an entry. There is one page for every entry. The entries in this encyclopedia are on:

- animals
- plants
- dinosaurs
- countries
- geography
- history
- world religions
- music
- art
- transport
- science
- technology

How to use this encyclopedia

This encyclopedia has eleven books, called volumes. The first ten volumes contain entries. The entries are all in alphabetical order. This means that Volume One starts with entries that begin with the letter 'A' and Volume Ten ends with entries that begin with the letter 'Z'. Volume Eleven is the index volume and has some other interesting information in its Fact Finder section.

Here are two entries, showing you what you can find on a page:

This is the letter that the entry starts with.

Fact boxes give you details about the topic.

The See also line tells you where to find other related information.

Did You Know? boxes have fun or interesting bits of information.

The Fact File tells you important facts and figures.

Libya

See also: Africa, Desert

Libya is a country in north Africa. It is mostly flat with a few low mountains. It is nearly all desert. It is cooler at the coast where it sometimes rains a little.

Living and working

Most of the people in Libya live in cities on the coast. A lot of oil and natural gas were discovered in 1959. So, Libya has become a very rich country.

Farms in the northern area grow dates, olives, citrus fruits, grapes and wheat. Sheep, goats, cattle and camels graze where there is enough for them to eat.

Libya is very dry. The people need more water for farming, drinking and washing. Because there are no rivers that flow all the year round, Libya is trying to bring water under ground from one end of the country to the other.

These Tuareg men in Southern Libya are performing a traditional dance.

DID YOU KNOW?

The highest temperature ever recorded was in Libya, in 1922. It was 58°C!

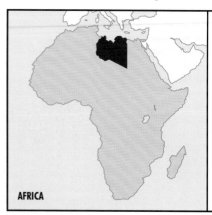

AFRICA

FACT FILE

PEOPLE........................Libyans

POPULATION................5.2 million

MAIN LANGUAGES........ Arabic, Berber, Italian, English

CAPITAL CITY..............Tripoli

MONEY.......................Libyan dinar

HIGHEST MOUNTAIN....Bette Peak – 2286 m

LONGEST RIVER .... Rivers run only when it rains.

Lice

See also: Insect

Lice are small insects. They have no wings, and they have very fat bodies. Lice live in the clothes, hair, feathers and fur of people and animals.

Lice families

An adult female louse lays tiny eggs, called nits. The nits take a week or two to hatch. Head-lice spread quickly in places where there are lots of people, such as schools. They move easily from person to person. They can make the skin and head itch.

LICE FACTS

NUMBER OF KINDS	3300
COLOUR	brown or yellow brown
SIZE	2.5–3.5 mm long
STATUS	common
LIFE SPAN	one month
ENEMIES	special chemicals, called insecticides

Tube for sucking up blood

Body swells up with blood

Claws for gripping hair and fur

A human head-louse

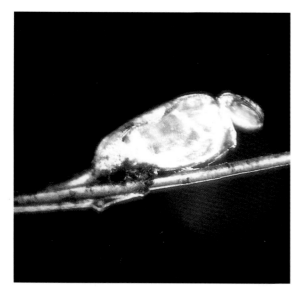

A head-louse egg on a human hair.

FOOD

Lice use their mouth tubes to prick a hole through the skin of their victims. Then they suck up blood. There are different sorts of lice that live on humans, some other mammals and some birds.

Life cycle

See also: Flower, Metamorphosis

A life cycle is all the stages in the life of an animal or plant. It includes the start of life, the process of growing, having young and then dying. Different living things have different stages to their life cycles.

Plant life cycle

Flowering plants start their life cycle as a seed. The baby plant grows in the seed. The baby plant grows leaves and roots, and gets bigger. When the new plant flowers, its male pollen can transfer to the female part of flower. A new fruit with a seed then grows.

DID YOU KNOW?

- Most insects have four parts to their life cycle: egg, larva, pupa, adult.
- Some insects, like grasshoppers, have only three stages: egg, nymph, adult.
- Amphibians have three stages as well: eggs, tadpoles, adults.
- Reptiles and birds lay eggs that hatch and the young grow into adults.

Human life cycle

Humans have a life cycle like most other mammals. A human starts as an egg in a female's body. The fertilized egg grows into a baby inside the mother. This takes about 40 weeks. After the baby is born it is cared for by its parents. At first it is fed on its mother's milk or on a milk substitute. As it grows, it learns to eat ordinary food.

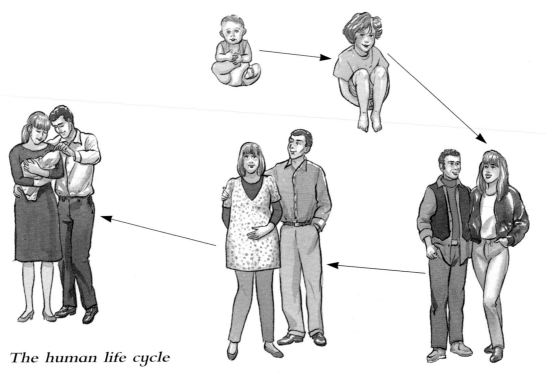

The human life cycle

Light

See also: Colour, Energy, Sun

Light is a form of energy. It helps us to see. We can only see things when light bounces off them and into our eyes.

The Sun and light

Light on Earth comes from the Sun. All of the food eaten on Earth depends on light from the Sun. All of the kinds of light we use when the Sun is not shining also depend on sunlight. Wood, gas, and electricity are all made using fuel that comes from plants that grew in sunlight.

At night big cities are filled with bright lights.

The Sun is the source of all Earth's light energy.

How light works

Light always travels in straight lines. Nothing travels faster than light. The Sun is 150 million kilometres from the Earth, but it only takes eight minutes for light from the Sun to travel to the Earth. Light bounces off shiny surfaces such as mirrors and polished metal. This is called reflection. Mirrors reflect light. Rays of light bend when they pass into water or clear glass. This is called refraction.

Lightning

See also: Electricity, Weather

Lightning is a giant electric spark that makes a bright flash of light in the sky. Thunder is the noise that a lightning flash makes as the lightning heats the air it moves through. Because light moves faster than sound, we see the lightning flash before we hear the thunder.

What causes lightning?

Lightning comes from energy in big clouds. Some of the energy turns into electrical energy. Lightning strikes when the electrical energy jumps to the ground, or to another cloud. Lightning usually strikes buildings and tall trees. Tall buildings usually have lightning conductors on top of them. This keeps the building safe, sending the electric charge from lightning down a very thick wire into the ground.

Benjamin Franklin (1706–90)

Benjamin Franklin was an American scientist and politician. He showed that lightning was electricity by flying a kite in a thunderstorm. The lightning struck the kite, and came down the wet string. This was very dangerous so he was lucky not to have been killed!

STAY SAFE!

If you are caught in a thunderstorm:
- Don't stay in the open, or on hills.
- Find shelter inside a building or a car, *not* under trees.
- If you are swimming or boating, get out of the water and find shelter.
- Don't talk on the phone – unless it is a mobile with no wires attached.

A lightning strike.

Lion

See also: Africa, Cat, Mammal

A lion is a large member of the cat family. Lions are mammals. Most live on the hot, sunny plains of Africa. A few live in India. They are strong, fast hunters, but they sleep or rest for about 20 hours a day.

LION FACTS

COLOUR	light brown
LENGTH	up to 2.8 m
WEIGHT	up to 180 kg
STATUS	common
LIFE SPAN	about 20 years
ENEMIES	cheetahs, hyenas, people

Lion families

A male is called a lion and a female is called a lioness. A lioness will have two or three cubs at a time. Lions, lionesses and their cubs live together in a group called a pride. The pride will live and hunt in one area, called their territory.

Sharp teeth for eating meat

Hairy mane on males to make them look fierce, and for protection when fighting

Strong legs for running in short, fast bursts

Sharp claws for hunting

A lion

FOOD

A lion can eat 40 kg of meat – half the size of an adult man – in one go. It will then spend several days sleeping off the meal. Lions usually hunt for animals such as zebra, wildebeest and antelope.

A lioness is always on guard for enemies that might attack her cubs.

Literature

See also: Drama, Poem, Story

Literature is writing of any kind which is meant for other people to read. It may be stories, plays, poetry or information. Some languages have no written form and so have no literature.

The first literature

From the time that people started writing, they have used it for two main purposes. First, they wrote down what had happened, recording their history. Second, people also used writing to record stories, poems and messages, mostly to do with religion the afterlife.

These children are discussing the books they've been reading with the rest of their class.

Literature today

As more people learned to read and write, literature grew into many forms. Many famous writers have left stories, drama and poetry as books for people to read. People can also see plays in theatres, and listen to cassettes of stories and plays. There are many TV programmes and videos of works of literature. New literature can also be picked up on the internet.

DID YOU KNOW?

The earliest form of writing that did not use pictures was called cuneiform. It was invented in Sumeria in the Middle East about 4000 years ago.

Cuneiform writing was made on clay tablets. This was the first literature.

Lizard

See also: Reptile

The lizard is a reptile. There are many kinds of lizards all over the world. Most are small, but a few, like monitor lizards, are large. The Komodo dragon is three metres long. Some lizards climb trees. Others live on the ground.

LIZARD FACTS

NUMBER OF KINDS	3700
COLOUR	usually greeny-brown
LENGTH	12 cm–3 m
WEIGHT	50 g–60 kg
STATUS	some are rare or threatened
LIFE SPAN	6–50 years
ENEMIES	snakes, birds, larger lizards

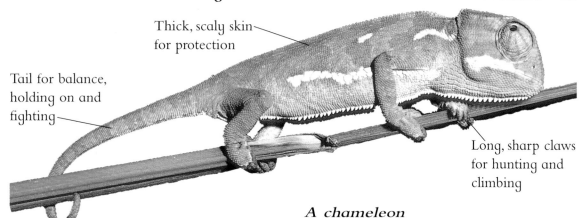

Thick, scaly skin for protection

Tail for balance, holding on and fighting

Long, sharp claws for hunting and climbing

A chameleon

This marine iguana baby rides on its mother when she climbs.

Lizard families

Some female lizards find good places to lay their eggs in soil. It needs to be warm enough to keep the eggs at the right temperature. After a few weeks the babies hatch. Other lizards keep the eggs inside them until they are ready to hatch.

FOOD

Lizards use their tongues to taste the air as they look for food. Most lizards eat insects and plants, but large lizards eat mammals.

Lung

See also: Air, Human body, Oxygen

Lungs are the organs that people and animals use for breathing. Lungs take oxygen out of the air. Carbon dioxide is in the used air that is breathed out.

Breathing

Breathing in air is called inhaling. Breathing out is called exhaling. The air that is inhaled through the nose and mouth is pushed in and out of the lungs using the muscles in the chest. Special hairs in the nose catch dust so it doesn't get to the lungs. The air goes down the windpipe into either lung. Air goes through smaller and smaller tubes in the lungs.

At the end of the small tubes, there are many tiny air sacs, called alveoli. Lots of blood goes to the alveoli to collect oxygen from the lungs and get rid of carbon dioxide.

Lung problems

Dirt and pollution can harm the lungs. Coughing is caused by the lungs squeezing together to get rid of the dirt inside.

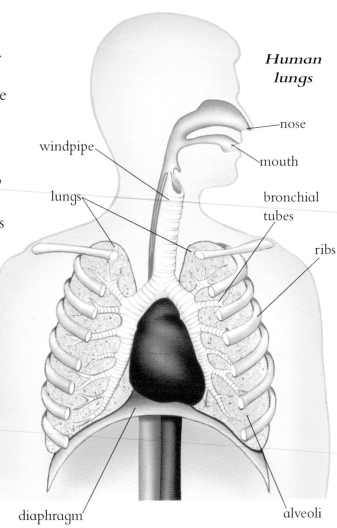

Human lungs

nose

mouth

windpipe

bronchial tubes

lungs

ribs

diaphragm

alveoli

DID YOU KNOW?

If the alveoli from both lungs of an adult were flattened out, they would cover a space the size of a tennis court.

STAY SAFE!

Keep your lungs healthy by never smoking cigarettes. If you are doing a dirty job, wear a mask. Try not to walk along main roads where you will breathe in exhaust fumes from cars, buses and lorries.

Luxembourg

See also: Europe

Luxembourg is one of the smallest countries in Europe. It is mostly hills and high, flat land. One third of the country has forests. Most of the rest is used for growing grass or crops. The summer months are warm, but winter can be cold, with snow.

Living and working

Almost all of the people in Luxembourg work in the towns and cities. There are factories making steel, glass, car tyres and chemicals. Most people work in banks and other office jobs.

Luxembourg has a royal family headed by the Grand Duke. Tourists come to Luxembourg to visit old towns and castles, and to see the landscape.

The flower market in Luxembourg.

DID YOU KNOW?

Luxembourg City is the headquarters for the European Court of Justice.

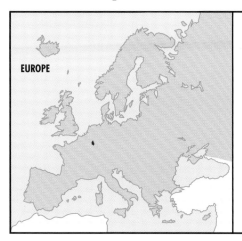

EUROPE

FACT FILE

PEOPLE.................. Luxembourgers

POPULATION............ 401,000

MAIN LANGUAGES.... Letzeburgish, French, German

CAPITAL CITY......... Luxembourg City

MONEY.................. Luxembourg franc

HIGHEST MOUNTAIN............. Buurgplaatz – 559 m

LONGEST RIVER....... River Moselle – 515 km

Machines, simple

See also: Energy

A machine is something that can help people to do work quickly or easily. When the parts of a machine move they can push or pull, or turn a small movement into a big movement. Here are six simple machines. All big, complicated machines are based on one or more of these.

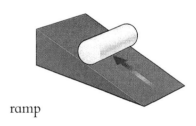
lever

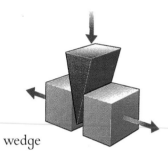
wedge

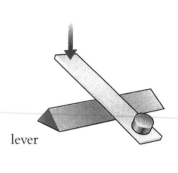
ramp

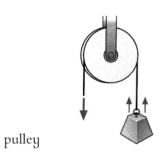
pulley

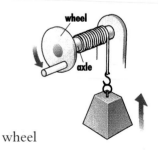
wheel
axle
wheel

screw

The different types of simple machines.

DID YOU KNOW?

Play equipment such as slides, swings and see-saws are simple machines.

Madagascar

See also: Africa, Island

Madagascar is an island country off the east coast of Africa. It is the world's fourth biggest island. There are mountains in the middle of Madagascar. Most of the low land and rivers are in the west. There are some rainforests. Along the east coast, there are coral reefs. The weather is mostly hot and wet.

Living and working

About three-quarters of the people in Madagascar live in the country and work on farms. Farmers grow rice, vegetables and fruit. People who live on the coast go fishing. They spend their time growing or catching the food they eat. Rice and vegetables are the main foods. Most food is cooked with hot spices, peppers and strong sauces. Coffee, cloves and vanilla are grown in Madagascar to sell to other countries.

This part of the market in Mahajanga sells fruit and vegetables.

DID YOU KNOW?

Madagascar is very important for its wildlife. There are 150,000 animals on the island that are not found anywhere else in the world. The most famous is the lemur, which is related to the monkey.

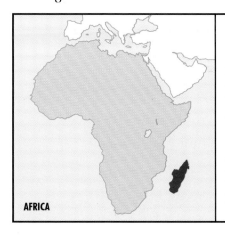

AFRICA

FACT FILE

PEOPLE .... Malagasy
POPULATION .... 14.3 million
MAIN LANGUAGES .... Malagasy, French
CAPITAL CITY .... Antananarivo
MONEY .... Malagasy franc
HIGHEST MOUNTAIN .... Mount Maromokotro – 2876 m
LONGEST RIVER .... River Mangoky – 560 km

Magnet

See also: Metal

A magnet is a piece of metal (usually iron or steel) that can pull another metal towards it. Every magnet has two ends called poles. One pole of a magnet is pulled towards the Earth's North Pole. This is the magnet's north pole. The other end is the magnet's south pole.

How magnets work

If the ends of two magnets come close to each other, and the close poles are both the same, the magnets push each other away. This is called repulsion. If the two poles are different, the magnets pull on each other. This is called attraction.

The Earth itself is a giant magnet. A compass has a magnetic needle that can turn around to point to the Earth's North Pole.

This horseshoe-shaped magnet can pick up metal objects, like a paperclip.

DID YOU KNOW?

A magnet can be used to tell if a can is made from steel or aluminium. Steel cans will stick to a magnet, but aluminium cans won't.

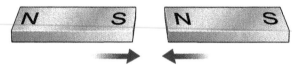

This shows which poles on magnets cause attraction and which cause repulsion.

How magnets are used

Permanent magnets can be used in many ways:

- Magnets can be used as door catches.
- Recording tapes and computer disks are magnetic. There are millions of tiny magnets mixed into the plastic.
- Radios, televisions and hi-fis all have magnets in the speakers where the sound comes out.
- Hospitals use magnets in a machine that can see through human bodies and make pictures like X-rays.

Malaysia

See also: Asia, Rainforest

The country of Malaysia has two parts. One part is on the south-east tip of Asia. The other part is on the north of the island of Borneo. Both parts are mostly forest with mountains. The climate is hot and wet.

Living and working

Half of the people in Malaysia live in the countryside. The farms grow rice, cocoa and palm nuts. People living by the coasts catch fish. There are many trees in the Malaysian rainforest. Some are cut down for their wood. Other trees have the rubber sap taken out of them. There are also factories where cars, electronic products and other things are made.

DID YOU KNOW?

The houses in Malay villages are called *kampongs*. They are made of wood and have roofs made from palm leaves.

These women are drying cuttlefish to sell as food.

The people of Malaysia are Malays, Chinese and people from India. Malaysia's food, houses and clothing come from all three cultures. The most well-known Malay food is *satay*. This is grilled meat on a stick, usually served with spicy, peanut sauce.

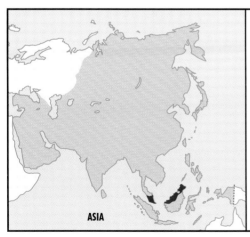

ASIA

FACT FILE

PEOPLE	Malays or Malaysians
POPULATION	19.7 million
MAIN LANGUAGES	Malay, Chinese
CAPITAL CITY	Kuala Lumpur
MONEY	Ringgit
HIGHEST MOUNTAIN	Kinabalu – 4101 m
LONGEST RIVER	River Rajang – 563 km

Mammal

See also: Animal, Vertebrate

Mammal is the name given to the group of animals that feed on their mother's milk when they are born. There are more than 4000 different kinds of mammal.

What makes a mammal?

All mammals have hair or fur. Most mammal babies are born alive out of the mother, not as eggs. Like other animals, mammals make heat using the energy from the food they eat. Because of this, mammals are called warm-blooded animals.

The smallest mammal is the shrew, like this one, which weighs only two grams.

Where do mammals live?

Mammals have lived on Earth since the time of the dinosaurs. Each mammal's body is different, to suit its way of life. For example, polar bears have thick, warm coats of white fur. They live in the freezing, snowy Arctic. Around the world, there are mammals living on the ground, in the trees and in the water. Some mammals, called bats, can even fly.

DID YOU KNOW?

The largest living mammal is the blue whale. It weighs over 100 tonnes and is 31 metres long.

There are only two mammals that lay eggs – the platypus and spiny echidnaes, like this.

Map

A map is a drawing of the land as it would look from above. A map that shows a very small area in great detail is called a plan. Charts are maps of the seas and oceans.

Using maps

Most maps are drawn for a special reason. Some maps only show roads. They help people to travel from one place to another. There are also weather maps and maps of the stars in the sky. Maps can be bound in a book called an atlas or printed on large sheets of paper that can be folded for carrying around. A globe is a round map of the whole world.

People use maps to find their way around an unfamiliar place.

What's on a map?

Maps of all kinds have three special things in common. They have a compass point. This shows the north, south, east and west directions on the map. They have a distance scale. This shows how far it is from one place to another on the map. Most importantly, they have a key or legend. This gives the meaning of all the signs and symbols on the map.

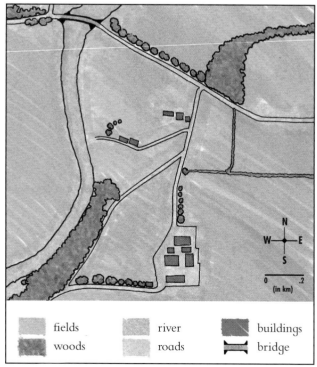

N
W ← → E
S

0   .2
(in km)

| | fields | | river | | buildings |
| | woods | | roads | | bridge |

This simple map shows a river, roads and some buildings.

Marsupial

See also: Australia, Kangaroo, Koala, Opossum

Marsupials are mammals. Female marsupials have pockets, called pouches, for their babies to live in. Kangaroos and koalas are marsupials. Marsupials are found in Australia, Papua New Guinea, North America and South America.

Marsupial babies

All marsupial babies are born very small, hairless and blind. After a marsupial baby is born, it has to crawl through the mother's fur and into her pouch. Once in the pouch, it stays there, drinking milk and growing until it is big enough to live outside.

Baby kangaroos, called joeys, are only about 2 cm long when they are born. When the joey gets big enough, it can hop in and out of its mother's pouch while she eats. When opossum babies get too big for the pouch, they ride on their mother's back.

MARSUPIAL FACTS

NUMBER OF KINDS	250
LARGEST	The red kangaroo can weigh up to 90 kg.
SMALLEST	The pilbra ningaui weighs only 2 g.
FASTEST	The kangaroo can bound along at 60 kph.

The brush-tailed possum is a marsupial from Australia. It is related to the American opossum.

The kangaroo joey lives in its mother's pouch. It will soon be too big to get in and out.

Matter

See also: Temperature

Matter is what everything around us is made of. All matter on Earth is in one of three forms. These are solid, liquid and gas.

Solids, liquids and gases

- Solids keep their shape and size. They cannot be squashed into a smaller space or stretched into a bigger space.
- All liquids can be poured. They change their shape to fit whatever container they are poured into.
- Gases can change their shape. They spread out to fill any space they are in.

Most matter can exist in all three forms at different times. For example, when frozen, water is ice, which is a solid. At a temperature between 0°C and 100°C, water is liquid. When it is heated to over 100°C, water turns into steam, which is a gas.

Here is water in its three states – liquid water, solid ice and the steamy gas.

DID YOU KNOW?

All matter is made of very small particles that are too small to see. These particles are called atoms. Most matter is made up of a combination of different atoms.

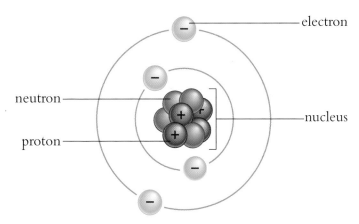

The parts of an atom

electron
neutron
proton
nucleus

Maya

See also: Aztecs, Hieroglyphics, Incas, Pyramid

The Maya were a Native American people who lived about 1500 years ago. They ruled parts of what is now Central America. The Maya took over many small groups of peoples, to form one big country. This was called the Mayan Empire. They were most powerful between AD 300 and AD 900.

DID YOU KNOW?

The Mayan priests invented a calendar of 365 days that was more accurate than the calendar used in the rest of the world for many years.

What were the Maya like?

The Maya were organized into small groups, each with their own king. One person might have ruled all the groups. There were also priests, warriors, traders and ordinary people – mostly farmers who grew crops in the fields. The Maya believed in many gods and goddesses who controlled the world.

KEY DATES

1500 BC..........The first Maya groups settled in what is now Mexico

AD 300–900... The Maya Empire grew. Cities were built. There was lots of trade

AD 900........... Something made the Mayan groups break up

AD 1520......... The Spanish moved into the area

Mayan step pyramids, like this one, were used to worship the gods and goddesses.

What are the Maya famous for?

The Maya are famous for their stone step pyramids and also for their beautiful pottery. They are also famous for their hieroglyphics (picture writing).

What happened to the Maya?

The Mayan Empire began to fall apart in about AD 900. No one knows why this happened. Other tribes may have invaded them. Some Mayan peoples moved south and were taken over by the Spanish. There are still Mayan Indians in most of the countries in Central America.

Measurement

See also: Calendar, Number, Time

Measurement describes the size of an object, or the number of things in a group. Measurements can be used to make things the right size. Using measurement, cakes and medicines can be made the same, every time.

The first measurements

The first measurements were units that could be found anywhere. In Ancient Egypt, measurements were made using parts of the human body. For example, a cubit was the length of the forearm, from the tip of the middle finger to the elbow. The problem with using parts of the human body is that not everyone is the same size.

The metric system

About 200 years ago the metric system was introduced in France. It has spread throughout the world.

DIFFERENT METRIC UNITS
Length: Kilometres (km), metres (m), centimetres (cm), millimetres (mm). 10 mm = 1 cm 100 cm = 1 m 1000 m = 1 km
Mass: tonnes (t), kilograms (kg), grams (g), milligrams (mg). 1000 mg = 1 g 1000 g = 1 kg 1000 kg = 1 t
Capacity: litres (l), millilitres (ml) 1000 ml = 1 l
Time: seconds, minutes, hours, days, months. 60 seconds = 1 minute 60 minutes = 1 hour 24 hours = 1 day 28–31 days = 1 month 12 months = 1 year

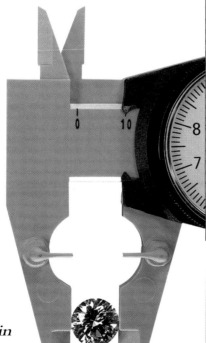

This diamond is being held in a gauge that measures carats.

DID YOU KNOW?

Some old units are still used for special things. The weight of diamonds are measured in carats. This is based on the weight of a carob bean.

Metal

See also: Rock

Metals are solid materials. They can be made into many different shapes. Some metals are strong, shiny and hard. Most metals are found in the ground, as part of rocks. These rocks are called ores.

Properties of metals

All metals let electricity and heat pass through them. This is called conduction. For example, most electric wires are made of copper. It conducts electricity and can be bent and stretched into wires.

Metals can be mixed together. This makes an alloy. The alloy can have the best properties of the metals it is made from. Bronze is an alloy of copper and tin. This alloy is stronger than both the other metals it is made from.

DID YOU KNOW?

Potassium is a soft metal, only as hard as cheese. It bursts into flames if it touches water.

Gold is a very valuable metal. It has been used for thousands of years to make jewellery and other objects. The mask of the mummy of the Egyption pharaoh Tutankhamen is made of gold.

Using metals today

The most important metals today are iron alloys, copper and aluminium. Many alloys containing iron are called steel. Steel is very strong. It is used in skyscrapers, ships and cars. Aluminium is quite strong, but is much lighter than steel. It can easily be bent into different shapes, like saucepans and drink cans.

The production of steel. Steel is being rolled into shape while red-hot in this steel works.

Metamorphosis

See also: Amphibian, Insect, Life cycle

Metamorphosis means 'change'. This word is used to describe how some insects, such as butterflies, go through different stages. A butterfly begins life as a tiny egg. It then turns into a caterpillar. When it comes out of its chrysalis it is a butterfly with beautiful wings.

The life cycle of a butterfly

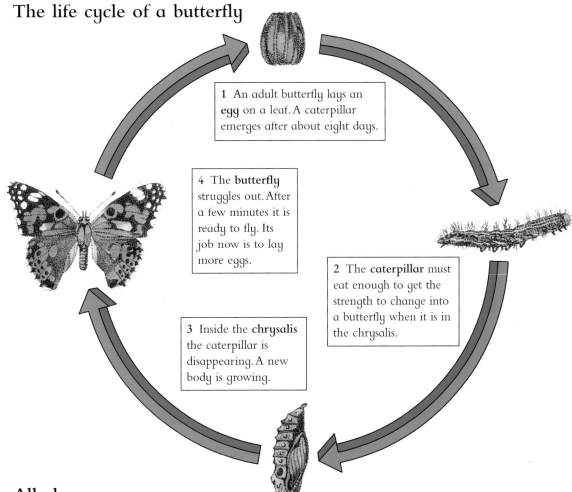

1 An adult butterfly lays an **egg** on a leaf. A caterpillar emerges after about eight days.

4 The **butterfly** struggles out. After a few minutes it is ready to fly. Its job now is to lay more eggs.

2 The **caterpillar** must eat enough to get the strength to change into a butterfly when it is in the chrysalis.

3 Inside the **chrysalis** the caterpillar is disappearing. A new body is growing.

All change

All insects and some amphibians go through a metamorphosis. For insects like butterflies this change is complete and sudden. For others such as grasshoppers the change is slower.

A grasshopper will change its skin four or five times as it grows. Each time it becomes more like an adult grasshopper. The new skin is soft and wet to begin with, but it hardens up as the air dries it.

Meteor

See also: Earth, Planet, Solar system

A meteor is a piece of rock or metal that flies through space. Meteors are sometimes called shooting stars. Most look like a tiny bright dot streaking across the sky.

Watching for meteors

Meteors can often be seen in the sky on a clear, dark night. A bright meteor may leave a glowing trail behind it. As the Earth moves through space it meets millions of meteors every day. Some meteors occur in groups, called meteor showers. These often come from the tails of comets.

DID YOU KNOW?

Some meteor showers can be seen at the same time every year. Most meteor showers last for a few days.

This meteorite crater in Arizona is more than a kilometre across. It was made about 25,000 years ago.

As a meteor enters the Earth's atmosphere it burns up. This causes the bright streak of light in the sky.

Meteorites

Meteorites are large pieces of rock or metal that come from space. They don't completely burn up in the atmosphere. They may be pieces of comets, of the other planets or they may come from other solar systems. When a big meteorite hits the ground very hard, the hole it makes is called a crater. Billions of years ago when the Earth formed many giant meteorites hit the ground. Most of their craters have been worn down by wind and rain, or filled with water. The moon has been hit by meteorites, and their craters can still be seen.

Mexico

See also: Aztecs, Maya, North America

Mexico is a country in North America. There are mountains in the west and near the Gulf of Mexico. Warm, dry, high flat land lies between. The coastal lowlands are hot and wet.

DID YOU KNOW?

Mexico City is built on top of the Aztec city of Tenochtitlàn. This was a city on an island in a lake.

Living and working

Many people live in the crowded cities and work in the factories. In the countryside, farmers grow maize, beans and vegetables for their families. Big farms grow cotton, coffee and fruit to sell in Mexico and to other countries.

The Mexican people are a mixture. There are the Native Indians who have lived in the area for thousands of years and people who came from Spain much later. So some of the food, like *enchilladas*, come from the old Indian cultures.

Mexicans can buy almost anything from the open markets found in most towns. This stall is selling fruit and vegetables.

NORTH AMERICA

FACT FILE

PEOPLE.................... Mexicans

POPULATION .... 92 million

MAIN LANGUAGE .... Spanish

CAPITAL CITY .... Mexico City

MONEY .... Peso

HIGHEST MOUNTAIN.............. Orizaba – 5700 m

LONGEST RIVER....... Rio Bravo Del Norte – 2092 km

Middle Ages

See also: Castle, Cathedral, Knight

The Middle Ages is the time in the history of Europe that comes between the fall of the Roman Empire and the Renaissance.

What happened in the Middle Ages?

At the beginning of the Middle Ages, each country was broken up into areas, all ruled locally. As the Middle Ages went on, most of Europe became Christian. The Church helped to unite Europe. People began to build towns and cities. They traded with each other more and fought less. The whole of Europe became richer. Castles, cathedrals and universities were built. At the beginning of the Middle Ages only people who were part of the Church could read and write. By the end, many more people could.

What happened next?

The Middle Ages did not suddenly stop. One by one, countries moved into the time called the Renaissance.

By the end of the Middle Ages more people lived in towns and cities. These people are making hay outside the city walls.

KEY DATES

AD 476 ..... The fall of the Roman Empire	AD 1100 ... The first universities are set up
AD 800 ..... The mainland of Europe unites under Emperor Charlemagne	AD 1130 ... The first school for doctors opens
AD 1066 ... William of Normandy conquers England	AD 1330 ... The Renaissance begins in Italy
	AD 1450 ... The Renaissance spreads through Europe

Migration

See also: Animal

Migration is a kind of journey made by an animal. It can be a journey to find a mate and breed. It can be to find food, or the right kind of weather. Many different kinds of animal migrate. People sometimes migrate, too.

DID YOU KNOW?

No one really knows how animals work out where to migrate. Birds seem to have a built-in compass. They are able to fly the right way even in the dark. Salmon seem to smell the rivers where they were born.

Why migrate?

Most migrating animals leave an area as winter approaches and travel to a warmer place. There they may have longer days and plenty of food to feed themselves and their young. Then, they return to where they came from. When they return they will breed.

Young salmon swim out to sea from the rivers where they were born. They stay in the sea for a year or two. This salmon is returning to where it was born. It has to swim against the current up a river to get back home.

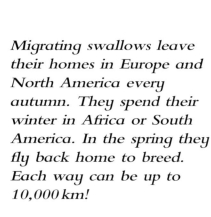

Migrating swallows leave their homes in Europe and North America every autumn. They spend their winter in Africa or South America. In the spring they fly back home to breed. Each way can be up to 10,000 km!

Mining

See also: Metal, Rock

Mining means digging things out of the Earth. Most mining is for rocks, minerals, metals, oil, gas and coal.

Types of mining

Rocks that are found near the surface of the ground can be dug from a pit. This is called open-cast mining. Giant mechanical shovels scoop up the rocks. Other things are mined deep underground. A mine shaft is dug down until it reaches the layer to be mined. Then explosives, drills and giant cutters are used to do the mining. Oil and gas are mined by drilling holes down into the ground. Then the oil or gas comes up to the surface on its own, or is pumped up.

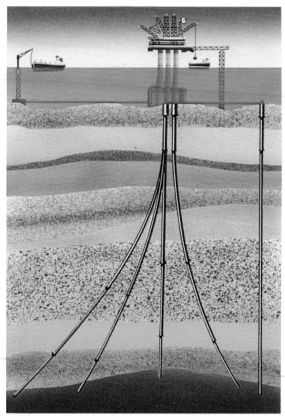

Oil and gas can be mined at sea from special platforms called rigs. The oil and gas is pumped up from deep under the sea floor.

Copper is being mined from this open-cast mine in Arizona, USA.

People and mining

For thousands of years, people have dug mines to get things they want. Salt is mined, to use in cooking and preserving food. Coal, gas and oil are mined and used for warmth, electricity and power for transport.

DID YOU KNOW?

Some precious metals and rocks are used to make jewellery. Silver, gold, diamonds and rubies all come from mines.

Mollusc

See also: Animal, Invertbrate

Molluscs are animals with soft bodies. They are invertebrates. There are over 70,000 different kinds of mollusc. Some molluscs have shells. The shells of cuttlefish and squid are inside their bodies.

Mollusc families

Different kinds of mollusc have different family lives. All molluscs lay eggs. Most female molluscs lay eggs on plants or in the water, and then leave them there. When the eggs hatch, the babies can find food for themselves without any help from their parents. Some molluscs do look after their eggs. The female giant octopus protects her eggs for six months before they hatch, never leaving her nest, even to find food for herself.

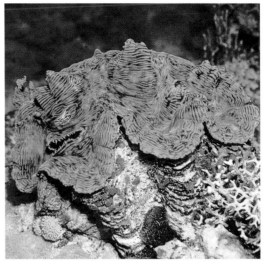

This large clam lives on the seabed off the coast of Australia.

Where molluscs live

Some molluscs, like some kinds of snails and slugs, live all their lives on land, crawling over and eating leaves. Squid and octopuses live in saltwater seas and eat fish and other water creatures.

Shellfish, which live on rocks under the sea, filter tiny animals and plants, called plankton, from the seawater. In rivers and lakes, there are freshwater clams and oysters that eat tiny freshwater creatures.

DID YOU KNOW?

The largest mollusc in the world is the giant squid, which can grow as long as 12 m. That is the length of a bus.

There are eight plates in the shell of this chiton.

Money

See also: Metal, Numbers

Money is used by people to buy things they need. People are given money in exchange for things they sell or for work they do.

Why use money?

Hundreds of years ago, people did not use money. They swapped things with each other instead. This was called bartering. People used shells, cocoa beans or bits of metal. It was easier than bartering.

Real money

The first proper money was in the form of metal coins. Later, governments began to make paper money. Every country has its own money. The coins and paper money look different and have different names.

Plastic money

A credit card is a plastic card that can be used to pay for something. The company that issues the card gives the shop the money later. Then it collects the money from the person who used the card. Many people call credit cards 'plastic money'.

Here is some money from different countries: Uganda, Brazil, USA, UK and Australia

DID YOU KNOW?

Cheques are a kind of money. They can be filled in with what ever amount is needed. But the person using the cheque has to have that money saved in the bank.

Monkey

See also: Ape, Mammal

A monkey is a mammal that is good at climbing and running. Monkeys have very strong arms and legs. They belong to the same group of mammals as apes and human beings. They live in Africa, Asia and South America.

Monkey families

Monkeys live in groups called troops. The biggest, strongest male monkey is the leader. Each troop will also have several female monkeys and their babies. A female monkey usually has only one baby at a time.

Strong tail to use as an extra arm for climbing and for balance

MONKEY FACTS

NUMBER OF KINDS	about 400
COLOUR	usually brown, black, white or grey
HEIGHT	12 cm–1 m
WEIGHT	70 g–45 kg
STATUS	some types are endangered
LIFE SPAN	up to 18 years
ENEMIES	birds, snakes, larger animals, people

Fur for keeping warm

Hands and feet have fingers and toes for holding on and picking things up

A baboon

FOOD

Monkeys move from place to place, eating fruit and leaves as they go. They peel fruit with their fingers and teeth. Some monkeys also eat insects and small mammals.

This baby squirrel monkey is with its mother and a brother or sister.

Moon

See also: Earth, Solar System, Space exploration, Sun

The Moon is a big ball of rock that travels around the Earth in a path called an orbit. It is the brightest thing in the night sky.

MOON FACTS

SIZE.................... 3500 km in diameter
DISTANCE .... 384,400 km from Earth
HOTTEST PART.... 127°C
COLDEST PART.... −173°C

The Moon's phases

Every month, the Moon goes through phases and seems to change shape. At first it looks like a thin crescent, then it seems to grow to a full circle, then shrink back again. The Moon takes about 29½ days for each of its orbits round the Earth.

It is always the same side of the Moon that faces the Earth. The Moon does not give out light itself, but is lit up by light from the Sun that reflects off its surface.

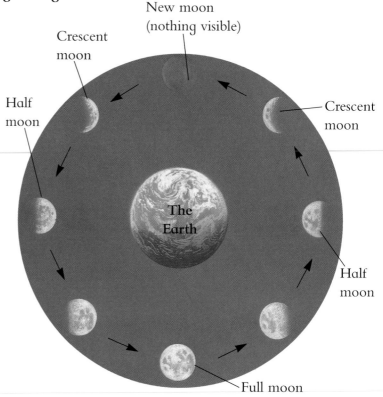

New moon (nothing visible)

Crescent moon

Half moon

Crescent moon

The Earth

Half moon

Full moon

The Moon only seems to change shape. This is because the light shining on it from the Sun gets blocked by the Earth. This picture shows you what the Moon looks like from Earth as an orbit takes place.

On the moon

The patterns on the moon are mountains, craters and plains. Most of the Moon's craters are billions of years old. There is no air or water on the Moon so the mountains and craters never wear away. In July 1969 the US spaceship Apollo 11 went to the Moon. The commander, Neil Armstrong, was the first person to walk on the Moon.

DID YOU KNOW?

Other planets in our solar system have moons that orbit them. Saturn has the most. It has 24 moons.

Moose

See also: Arctic, Deer, Tundra

The moose is the largest deer in the world. It is a mammal. The European moose is called an elk. Moose live in forests all over the northern part of the world. In summer moose often walk into lakes to eat water plants and to keep cool.

MOOSE FACTS

NUMBER OF KINDS	6
COLOUR	brown with lighter brown legs
LENGTH	up to 3 m
HEIGHT	up to 2.3 m
WEIGHT	400–800 kg
STATUS	common
LIFE SPAN	about 20 years
ENEMIES	wolves, cougars, people

Moose families

The male moose is called a bull. The female moose is called a cow. Male moose live on their own, but fight over females every autumn. The female moose has one or two babies in the spring. These babies, called calves, may stay with her for a year.

Thick, furry coat for keeping warm

Males have large antlers for fighting

Sensitive nose for smelling danger

Males have a growth of skin and hair known as a 'bell'

A male moose

FOOD

A moose eats only plants, including water plants and grass. Each moose eats many plants each day.

This female moose is grazing with her young calf.

Morocco

See also: Africa, Desert

Morocco is a country on the north-west coast of Africa. There are mountain ranges, a high, flat area and some desert. The coast has hot summers and mild, wet winters.

Living and working

Many people in Morocco live in the countryside. Most are farmers. They grow citrus fruit, vegetables, wheat and barley. Other people work in tourism, mining and fishing.

Moroccans eat a lot of a dish called *couscous*. It is made from wheat grown by farmers. The wheat is cracked and then cooked by steaming. Almost anything can be eaten with *couscous*, but stews made of spicy meat and vegetables are very popular.

Covered markets called bazaars can have whole streets of shops selling the same thing. This street sells items made of brass.

DID YOU KNOW?

Computers are being used to help farmers in Morocco. The computers are programmed to run machines that automatically water crops.

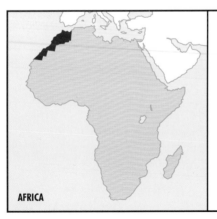

AFRICA

FACT FILE

PEOPLE .... Moroccans

POPULATION .... 26.5 million

MAIN LANGUAGES .... Arabic, Berber

CAPITAL CITY .... Rabat

MONEY .... Dirham

HIGHEST MOUNTAIN .... Jebel Toubkal – 4165 m

LONGEST RIVER .... Oued Moulouya – 570 km

Mosquito

See also: Fly, Insect

A mosquito is a small fly. It is an insect found all over the world. Mosquitoes like to live in warm and wet places. Many mosquitoes carry diseases.

Mosquito families

Mosquitoes don't look after their eggs or babies. A female mosquito lays her eggs in still or slow-flowing water.

MOSQUITO FACTS

NUMBER OF	
KINDS	3000
COLOUR	brownish
LENGTH	5–10 mm
STATUS	common
LIFE SPAN	less than one year
ENEMIES	birds, bats, people

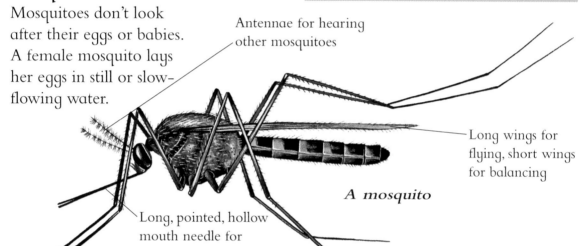

Antennae for hearing other mosquitoes

Long wings for flying, short wings for balancing

A mosquito

Long, pointed, hollow mouth needle for sucking blood or nectar

It takes three stages for a mosquito to grow from an egg to become an adult mosquito. The eggs hatch into little worm-like larvae, which live in the water. When a larva is fully-grown, it forms a covering to become a pupa, and then the adult mosquito comes out of the pupa.

FOOD

A mosquito larva feeds on tiny animals in the water. Adult female mosquitoes drink the blood of humans or animals. Male mosquitoes drink nectar or plant juice.

This mosquito is emerging from its pupa.

Moss

See also: Plant

A moss is a small, green plant that grows best in damp places. Mosses usually grow close together to form a mat. Mosses do not produce flowers. They grow all over the world, except in the sea. They are mostly found on smooth rocks, on trees and on the ground.

The life of a moss

A new moss plant grows in two stages. First a male sperm and female egg combine and grow into a long stalk with a capsule at the end. Inside the capsule are thousands of spores which may grow into new moss plants.

Many insects live in mosses, and birds sometimes line their nests with moss. Moss holds water like a sponge. This stops the water draining away. Peat is a spongy kind of soil which forms from the broken-down remains of peat moss.

Moss likes to grow in cool, dark places. This hair moss has green and red leaves.

MOSS FACTS

NUMBER OF KINDS	12,000
HEIGHT	up to 15 cm

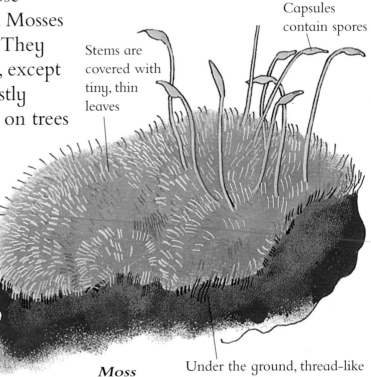

Stems are covered with tiny, thin leaves

Capsules contain spores

Under the ground, thread-like roots take in water and hold the moss in place

Moss

Moth

See also: Butterfly, Caterpillar, Insect, Metamorphosis

A moth is an insect with large wings. A moth begins its life as a caterpillar, and only changes into a moth later. Moths are found all over the world. Moths fly mostly in the evening or at night.

How moths live

When a moth caterpillar has eaten enough food to become very plump, it spins a cocoon around itself and becomes a chrysalis. Inside the chrysalis the caterpillar changes into an a moth.

Each kind of moth has a different way of avoiding enemies. The tiger moth tastes horrible to birds. The buff-tip moth looks like a twig. This helps it hide. The eyed-hawk moth has large eye patterns on its wings that frighten off enemies.

MOTH FACTS

NUMBER OF	
KINDS	over 100,000
SIZE	3 mm–20 cm across
STATUS	some species threatened
LIFE SPAN	up to 3 years
ENEMIES	birds, bats, reptiles, frogs, toads

A luna moth

Feelers to act like eyes and nose. Many moths find each other using their feelers and sense of smell

Tiny scales make up the colourful patterns

Veins hold the wings flat and strong for flying

FOOD

Moths sip the sweet juice from flowers and rotting fruit. They eat using a mouth tube. When they aren't drinking, they can roll it up.

The caterpillars have already hatched out of these fox moth eggs.

Motorcycle

See also: Bicycle, Transport

A motorcycle is a vehicle with two wheels. It carries one or two people, using energy from an engine to push it. Motorcycles were invented over a hundred years ago.

The first motorcycles

The first motorcycles were just bicycles fitted with an engine. They were very slow and quite dangerous. Later, more powerful engines were invented. Motorcycles with the new engines could go faster. Soon motorcycles could reach speeds of 160 kph. They were still very heavy and hard to steer. Lighter frames and engines, and softer tyres to absorb the bumps, made motorcycles more comfortable to ride.

Modern motorcycles can travel very fast. They also have room for a passenger to sit behind the driver.

At a motorshow in 1930, this motorcycle and sidecar were the latest thing. The passenger in the sidecar even had a sliding roof.

How motorcycles are used

All over the world motorcycles are used for transport. They don't get stuck in traffic and they use less fuel, so they are cheap to run. But motorcycle riders can get very cold in bad weather, and motorcycles are not very safe on icy roads or snow.

MOTORCYCLE FIRSTS

INVENTED	1869
FIRST PRODUCED	1885
FIRST TRACK RACES	1897
FIRST CROSS-COUNTRY RACE	1907

Mountain

See also: Continent, Island, Volcano

Mountains are areas of high land with steep, sloping sides. The highest point on a mountain is called the peak. A mountain is usually over 500 metres high. Most mountains are part of a large group called a mountain range or chain.

How mountains are made

Mountains are usually made when flat layers of rock are pushed by forces in the Earth. They can be pushed so much that they make giant ripples called folds. Some mountains are volcanoes. They grow bigger every time they erupt and molten rock flows out of them. Some mountains rise from the ocean bed. Their peaks make small islands.

DID YOU KNOW?

The 25 highest mountains in the world are all in the Himalayan and Karakoram mountain ranges, which are both in the same area of Asia. These mountains are still getting bigger.

People and mountains

Not many people live in high mountains. The land can be too steep and too cold and wet to grow crops. But people can enjoy ski-ing and other mountain sports, such as climbing. Mountains are also good places to build reservoirs to store water. Fast-flowing water running down mountains can be used to make electricity in power stations.

Mountains are used for winter sports like ski-ing and snowboarding.

Mouse

See also: Mammal

A mouse is a very small mammal, about as big as a chicken's egg. It is covered in fur, with a long, thin tail. The word 'mice' is used for more than one mouse. Mice have large front teeth for nibbling. They eat nuts and fruit.

Mouse families

A male mouse is called a buck and a female mouse is called a doe. Mouse cubs are born blind, deaf and hairless. Their eyes open after a week. One doe mouse can give birth to a hundred cubs in one year.

Tail to balance when running and climbing.

MOUSE FACTS

NUMBER OF	
KINDS..............	1082 mice and rats
COLOUR.........	brown, black, white
LENGTH..........	7–8 cm, with a tail as long again
STATUS	common
LIFE SPAN........	about 2 years
ENEMIES..........	cats, birds of prey, people
NUMBERS........	Mice are the third most common mammal.

Ears for good hearing

Eyes on the sides of the head for all-round vision

Claws for gripping

A harvest mouse

FOOD

Some wild mice moved in with humans about 10,000 years ago. Houses and farm buildings were warm places to live, with plenty of food. Mice like grains such as wheat, but will eat household scraps.

This is a nest of wood mice cubs. They will soon look like their mother.

Music

See also: Musical instrument

Music is making sounds using voices and instruments. No one really knows what very early music was like, but human beings have sung and chanted from earliest times.

Music around the world

There are many different kinds of music. Each part of the world has its own special kind of music, such as flamenco music from Spain and gamelan music from Indonesia. Today, many types of music are made and enjoyed all over the world, including pop music, classical music, folk and jazz.

India has had its own tradition of making music for hundreds of years. This Indian musician is playing an Indian stringed instrument called a sitar.

This picture shows the famous jazz musician Dizzy Gillespie playing his specially made trumpet. The trumpet is also used in popular and classical music.

Pythagoras (582–500 BC)

Some of the earliest ideas about music were those of the Ancient Greek philosopher Pythagoras. He discovered that the differences between musical notes could be worked out using numbers. This idea led to the way in which a lot of music is composed and written down today.

Musical instrument

See also: Music

Musical instruments are made especially for making music. They can be very simple, such as a triangle. They can be very complicated such as an electronic keyboard. Everyday objects, like a washboard or dried seed pod, can also be used as musical instruments.

Jimi Hendrix (1942–70)

Jimi Hendrix was an American musician. He played the electric guitar. Hendrix was always looking for new ways to make sounds. In one of his songs, he played a tune by humming through a comb covered in paper!

This Aboriginal Australian musician is using a stick to beat out a rhythm.

Jimi Hendrix played the electric guitar, which is a very popular modern instrument.

The first instruments

People started out using parts of their bodies to make sounds. They clapped their hands, stamped their feet and listened to the rhythm of their heartbeats. Sticks used to beat out rhythms were the first instruments.

Instruments today

Today instruments are grouped by the way they make sounds. Some use strings, some use the player's breath, some are hit or shaken and some use electronics to make sounds.

Myth

See also: Legend, Literature, Story

Myths are stories about gods, goddesses and spirits that people in the past believed in. Myths often try to explain how the world was created, or how important discoveries, such as fire, were made.

DID YOU KNOW?

Studying myths can help us learn about how people in the past thought.

Greek, Roman and Norse myths

The most famous myths are those of the Ancient Greeks and Romans, and the Norse myths of the Vikings. They explain how these ancient people saw the natural world. Most tell stories of how the gods and goddesses came down to Earth and played tricks or fell in love with human beings.

Natural things like thunder and lightning were often explained in myths as signs of the gods' anger.

This Native American ceremonial drum with a mythical bird painted on it was made by the Ojibwa tribe.

Myths of native people

The Native Americans, the Aborigines in Australia and the Maoris in New Zealand also have many myths. Different tribes have explanations in their myths for how things happened in the world. Most Native American myths are about the animals that represent the spirits of the Earth.

Native Americans

See also: Bison, North America, South America

The Native Americans were the first people of North America. They have been on the continent for about 40,000 years. Today there are 2.5 million Native Americans.

DID YOU KNOW?

The name 'Indian' was given to Native Americans by the first explorers from Europe. The explorers thought they had reached the area in Asia called the Indies.

Land and life

Native Americans divided into groups called tribes. In the north-east of America the Mohawk tribe lived in homes called longhouses. Many families shared the same longhouse. They grew maize, and hunted deer.

Some of the Native Americans lived in forests and used rivers as their roads.

Tribes like the Lakota lived on the grassy plains. They hunted bison. As the bison roamed, so did the Lakota. They lived in tents called *teepees.* The *teepee* could be taken apart and moved when the bison moved on.

Native Americans today

Most tribes had their land taken when European settlers arrived. Many were made to live in special areas called reservations. Some tribes, like the Navajo, have kept their old way of life.

Tribes that moved carried their belongings with them. This kind of bundle on poles is called a travois.

Nepal

See also: Asia, Mountain

Nepal is a small country in Asia. It is one of the world's highest countries because most of Nepal is in the Himalayan Mountains. Almost half of Nepal is covered with forests. It is warmer and wetter lower down in the valleys.

Living and working

Nearly everyone living in Nepal works on farms. Rice and vegetables are the most important crops. Some farmers raise goats, cattle and buffalo. They also cut down trees to sell the wood. People from the Sherpa tribe often work as mountain guides for tourists and visiting climbers.

Most Nepalese are Hindus. They believe in many gods and goddesses. People often celebrate holy days by washing in a river or lake. There is singing and dancing to celebrate weddings and farming events.

This cart is part of the Nepalese New Year festival.

DID YOU KNOW?

A Nepalese Sherpa called Tenzing Norgay and the New Zealand mountain climber, Sir Edmund Hillary, were the first people to reach the top of Mount Everest in the Himalayas. They reached the top of the world's tallest mountain on 29 May 1953 after climbing for two months.

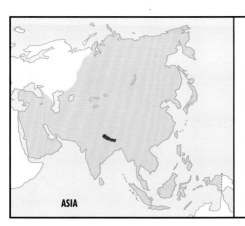

ASIA

FACT FILE

PEOPLE	Nepalese
POPULATION	21.4 million
MAIN LANGUAGE	Nepali
CAPITAL CITY	Katmandu
MONEY	Nepalese rupee
HIGHEST MOUNTAIN	Mount Everest – 8848 m
LONGEST RIVER	River Ghaghara – 920 km

Netherlands

See also: Europe

The Netherlands is a country in north-west Europe. It has a coast along the North Sea. Most of the Netherlands is low and flat. Land that used to be under water has been drained using walls called dykes and pumps. These areas are called polders.

Living and working

Dutch farmers grow crops and raise herds of dairy cows. Dutch cheese is sold in many countries. Some farmers grow tulips and other flowers. There are big factories in the ports of Rotterdam and Amsterdam.

Some of the world's most famous artists were Dutch. The painters Rembrandt, Van Gogh and Vermeer were all born in the Netherlands.

The Netherlands are famous for their tulips and their windmills. The windmills used to pump water away from flooded land. Now most pumping is done by big machines.

DID YOU KNOW?

People sometimes call this country Holland. One part of the Netherlands is called Holland, but this is not the correct name for the whole country.

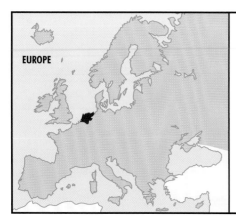

EUROPE

FACT FILE

PEOPLE.................Dutch, Netherlanders
POPULATION......... 15.4 million
MAIN LANGUAGE...Dutch
CAPITAL CITY........Amsterdam
MONEY.................Guilder
HIGHEST LAND......Vaalserberg – 321 m
LONGEST RIVER.....River Rhine – 1320 km